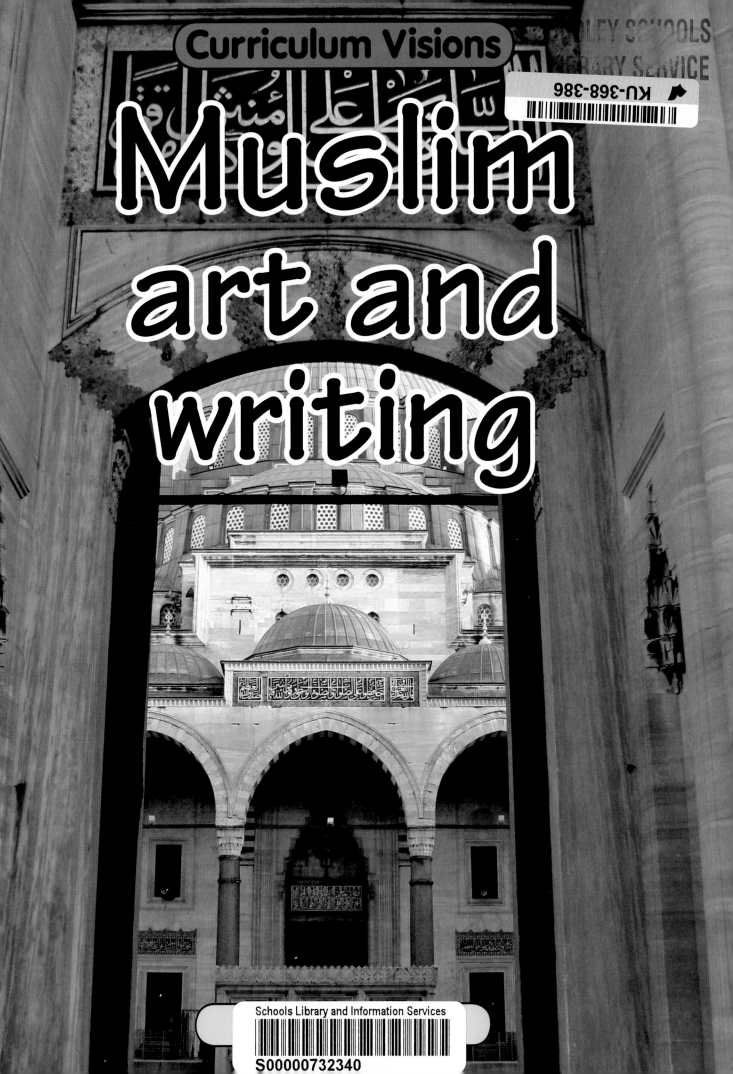

Curriculum Visions

Muslim art and writing

Glossary

CALLIGRAPHY Writing that has been made in a beautiful or fancy way, so that it is also art. The Qur'an is sometimes written in beautiful calligraphy, to show how important it is.

CHANTING Saying words or phrases in a rhythmic way to the same note or notes. Chanting does not use music.

GEOMETRIC DESIGN A design that is made up of shapes, such as circles, squares, lines or curves. The shapes are often in repeating patterns.

IMAM The leader of the religious community. Imams are usually people who have studied Islamic law and religion, often at Islamic universities or schools. The imam leads the prayers in the mosque and gives a sermon at the noon prayer on Fridays.

ISLAM The religion followed by Muslims. Islam is an Arabic word which means obedience. Islam is a set of beliefs and practices. Islamic beliefs include the belief in one God (Allah) and that the Prophet Mohammed (pbuh) was God's last prophet.

KA'BA A mosque in Mecca that Muslims believe was first built by Adam, and rebuilt by Abraham.

MIHRAB Muslims must always pray facing the city of Mecca. One wall of the prayer hall in the mosque always faces Mecca, and on the wall is a niche, called the mihrab.

MINARET A tall tower at the side of a mosque. This is where the muezzin chants the call to prayer.

MOSAIC A picture or design made by setting small coloured pieces, such as stone or tile, into a surface.

MOSQUE A building where Muslims go to pray and to be part of the Muslim community. Mosques can be large or small, plain or fancy.

MUEZZIN Muslims must pray five times each day, at certain times. Before there were clocks, a man would stand in the minaret and chant a phrase that would remind people it was time to pray. This is the call to prayer, or adhan. The person who chants the call to prayer is called a muezzin. Today, in many Muslims countries, muezzins still chant the call to prayer because it is a tradition.

MUSLIM A Muslim is a person who follows the Islamic religion. The word Muslim is an Arabic word which means "a person who obeys God". There are more than one billion Muslims around the world.

PILGRIMAGE It is the duty of every Muslim who can afford it to make a trip to Mecca at least once in their life at a certain time of year. This trip is called the pilgrimage, or Hajj. Once in Mecca, they perform a series of prayers and religious rituals that last several days.

PROPHET MOHAMMED (PBUH) The founder of Islam. He was born about fourteen centuries ago near the city of Mecca in what is now Saudi Arabia. Muslims believe that God sent many messages to the prophet Mohammed (pbuh). The prophet Mohammed (pbuh) then preached these messages to the people around Mecca. The words "peace be unto him", or the abbreviation "pbuh", are often placed after the prophet Mohammed's (pbuh) name, to show respect.

QUR'AN The holy book of Islam. Muslims believe that, during his lifetime, Mohammed (pbuh) received many messages from God. Because Mohammed (pbuh) could not write, he recited these messages to his followers, who memorised them. During Mohammed's (pbuh) lifetime, and after his death, the messages were written down to form the Qur'an.

SYMBOL An object, image, picture or letter that has a special meaning. Some symbols can have more than one meaning.

TAJ MAHAL A tomb, or mausoleum built by the ruler of India, Emperor Shah Jahan Mahal, for his favourite wife, Mumtaz Mahal. It is located in Agra, India, and was completed in 1648.

WUDU Before prayer, Muslims must wash their hands, feet, arms, face and neck in a certain way. This is called wudu.

Contents

Glossary.. 2

Muslim worship through art 4

Using designs to show faith 6

Tile mosaics 12

Symbols in Islamic
    art and worship 16

Making art with words.................. 20

The art of architecture.................. 24

Music for worship.......................... 30

Index.. 32

As you go through the book, look for words in **BOLD CAPITALS**. These words are defined in the glossary.

⚠️ Understanding others

Remember that other people's beliefs are important to them. You must always be considerate and understanding when studying about faith.

Muslim worship through art

Muslims use many different types of art to show their faith.

People show their faith in many ways, such as through prayer, but there are many other ways that people can express their faith, for example, through art. Art is anything that people create in order to express ideas, thoughts or feelings. Many people show their faith through arts such as painting, sculpture, drama or music. These ways of expression can be just as meaningful as prayer.

Art without people and animals

The Islamic faith teaches that people should worship only God.

Some of the early leaders of Islam felt that if a work of art, such as a painting or drawing, showed people or animals then people might accidentally worship the work of art instead of God. For example, if there were paintings of Mohammed (pbuh) in mosques, then people might accidentally worship the painting of Mohammed (pbuh) instead of worshipping God.

Because of this, many Muslims feel it is wrong to have paintings and sculptures that show people and animals in places of worship such as mosques.

For the same reason, Islamic religious art does not use images of people or animals no matter where it is displayed.

God created beauty

Muslim belief teaches that God created beauty and that God loves beauty. The Prophet Mohammed (pbuh), the founder of Islam, once said "God is beautiful and he loves beauty." So, Muslim artists try to show beauty in all of their art as a way of showing their love of God. Because they do not use pictures of people or animals, the artists use other ways to show the beauty of the world around them. For example, Islamic art uses designs and words in the most imaginative ways.

On the following pages we will learn more about this.

▼ This ancient Muslim tomb uses carvings of plant designs and words as decoration, instead of images of people or animals.

▼ Stained glass showing a geometric design.

Using designs to show faith

Designs and patterns may look simple, but they can have many different meanings.

Geometric designs, patterns and words can easily be used to show religious meaning. Geometric designs can be made up of simple straight lines, shapes like circles, squares and triangles, or more complicated shapes.

Repeating patterns

Islamic art often uses designs that repeat themselves over and over. In many Islamic designs, the design is also made so that each half is a mirror image of the other. This is called symmetry.

Muslims believe that God has always existed and always will exist. The repeating patterns are a reminder of this ideal – that God will never change or go away. At the same time, the designs are also a reminder that God's laws are unchanging and will last forever.

The meaning of different shapes

Some of the shapes used in Islamic designs can help to tell us about the Muslim faith.

For example, many patterns are made up of circles, or have circles in them. The circles are a reminder of God, because circles have no beginning or end, in the same way that God also has no beginning or end.

Some designs show a circle with another design in the centre. The design in the centre of the circle may be a reminder of the way that Mecca is at the centre of Islam, and how all Muslims face Mecca to pray.

The hexagonal shape is sometimes used to stand for Heaven.

▲ A design with a pattern of hexagons and stars.

▼ Mosaic designs in a mosque.

Another very important shape in Islamic design is the star. Because stars give off light, star shapes can be a reminder of the light of God. Stars were also very important to the first Muslims. These people lived in the desert and used the stars to help them find directions and to travel at night.

Muslims pray facing Mecca, and the stars also helped the first Muslims to find the direction of Mecca for the evening prayers. So, using star shapes in art can also be a reminder of the beginnings of Islam.

Making mistakes

Sometimes, Islamic artists put small mistakes into their designs. This is not an accident. It is done on purpose as a reminder that only God is perfect.

▲ A design in a mosque showing plants and geometric patterns.

Plant designs

Islamic art does not use only geometric designs. Many designs also use drawings or paintings of plants and flowers.

Just like with the geometric designs, plants are sometimes drawn so that they appear to go on forever. This is done by having the stems, flowers and leaves in the design wind around each other, so that you cannot tell where one plant begins and another one ends.

Other types of art show individual plants and flowers, or use plants as a border around words. This helps to highlight the words and make them look nicer.

Using plants in works of art may remind people of the garden of Eden, or the garden of paradise in Heaven. Or the plants may remind people that God created everything, including nature.

The type of flowers and plants used in the work of art may also have special meanings. For example, the cypress tree stands for mourning and also for the idea that after we die we are with God in Heaven. The palm tree and the coconut may stand for the blessing of God. The peony flower sometimes stands for wealth.

Using colours

Any colour can be used in Islamic art but sometimes colours can add meaning. For example, the colour green may be used as a reminder of Mohammed (pbuh), because green is said to have been his favourite colour. Green is also a reminder of the gardens of paradise or Heaven.

► **A decorative metal screen.**

In some parts of a mosque, plain colours, such as black or white, may be used in order to help people to concentrate on worship.

Designs for everyday objects

Geometric designs are also often used on plates and other types of dishes. Even though the dishes are used every day for non-religious purposes (eating), the designs help people to understand that God is everywhere, even at the dinner table. In the same way, geometric designs can have a useful purpose.

For example, one place that you can find geometric designs is in wooden, metal or stone screens. Hundreds of years ago, these screens were used on the outside of houses to let in light and let people see out, without allowing anyone to see in. Today they are used as decoration.

The carvings are also very useful for everyday living. The carvings on the screens help to give a feeling of space and light to houses. The holes let air and light into the house, while giving shade at the same time. As the air moves through the holes, it helps to cool the house. In hot climates, these screens were very good at cooling down houses. You can see that art can be useful in many ways.

11

Tile mosaics

Tile mosaics are used in mosques to help worshippers feel closer to God.

What are mosaics?

In ancient times, ceramic tiles were used to add colour and beauty to many types of buildings, such as mosques, palaces, government buildings and even homes. Today, many mosques still use ceramic tiles as decoration. The tiles are painted with designs and words and can be put together to form large patterns, called mosaics.

By looking at tile mosaics you can see how many different ideas of Islamic art, such as using geometric designs, images of plants and repeating patterns, can be put together to make art.

Different patterns

By placing identical tiles together, it is easy to make patterns that are connected and seem to go on forever.

▲ A mosaic of plants on a mosque.

Another type of mosaic pattern is made from tiles that look different from each other. By placing these tiles together artists can make new and interesting patterns and designs that are very colourful and decorative.

Mosaic tiles can also be used to make pictures. Each tile has a part of the picture on it, but the whole picture is only visible once all the tiles have been put together.

▶ Identical tiles make a seemingly never-ending pattern on a mosque in Saint Petersburg, Russia.

▲ Tiles on the outside of Sheikh Loft Allah Mosque in Isfahan, Iran.

Types of tile mosaics

There are many different ways to make tile mosaics. One way is to use tiles that are all the same shape, such as square. Another way that is often used in Islamic art is to use tiles that are all different shapes. The shapes are then fitted together to make geometric designs. This way of making mosaics is called tessellae, or tesserae.

Mosaic designs that tell stories

Mosaic designs can also be used to remind people of stories or teachings. For example, a design that looks like a spider's web or the branches of a rose bush may be a reminder of the story of "God's spider's web".

In this story, when the Prophet Mohammed (pbuh) fled from Mecca to escape his enemies, he and his companion, Abu Bakr, hid in a cave. The hostile Meccans rode out in search of them, and after three days they reached the entrance to the cave.

But during the three days, a spider had spun its web across the entrance to the cave, a dove had laid its eggs on the threshold, and a

▲ This pattern may be a reminder of the rose bush over the cave entrance in the story of Abu Bakr.

wild rose-bush had stretched out its blossoming branches. So the pursuers thought that no one could possibly have recently entered the cave. They turned around and rode away and Mohammed (pbuh) and Abu Bakr were saved.

Mosaic tiles in the mosque

Many mosques are decorated with mosaic tiles in colourful geometric designs that repeat over and over. The repeating designs can add a feeling of space to the mosque, because it is hard to tell where the design begins and ends. The designs are also a reminder that God goes on forever, just like the design.

▼ In most mosques, the mihrab is often covered in mosaic tiles or painted with geometric designs. This helps to show that the mihrab has a special importance in the mosque. As the part of the mosque that points towards Mecca, the mihrab is the main part of the prayer room.

Symbols in Islamic art and worship

Many different symbols are used in Islamic art.

A symbol is a design, drawing or object that can have special meaning. In the previous pages, we have seen how plants and designs can be used as symbols in Islamic art. On these pages we will look at some more symbols of Islam.

Crescent Moon and star

You will see a Crescent Moon and star on the outside of many mosques. When Islam began, most Muslims lived in the desert and relied on the Moon and stars to tell the time of month, time of year and to find direction at night. The Crescent Moon is a reminder of this time.

The Moon symbol is also a reminder that the Muslim calendar is based on the phases of the Moon, and Muslims use the Moon to find the times for important religious events and holidays.

The Crescent Moon shape is a reminder that all life comes and goes, just like the phases of the Moon. The Crescent Moon also reminds Muslims how Islam guides and lights their way through life, just like the Moon guided the first Muslims through the deserts.

▶ A star and Crescent Moon on the dome of a mosque are symbols of Islam.

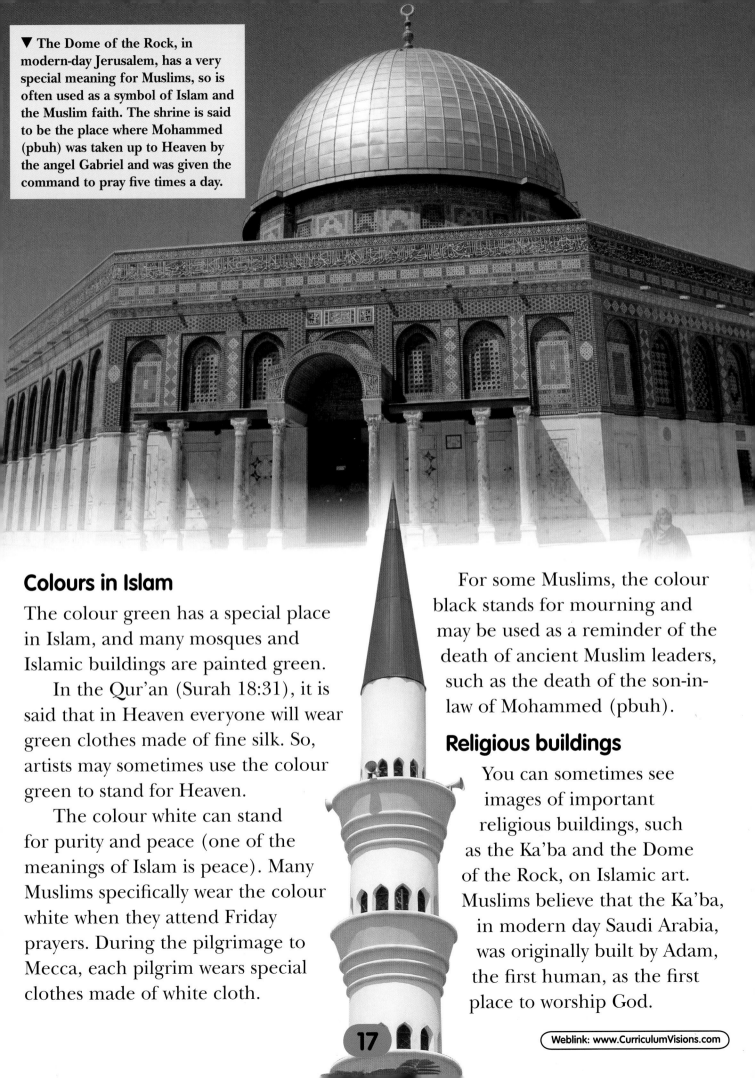

▼ The Dome of the Rock, in modern-day Jerusalem, has a very special meaning for Muslims, so is often used as a symbol of Islam and the Muslim faith. The shrine is said to be the place where Mohammed (pbuh) was taken up to Heaven by the angel Gabriel and was given the command to pray five times a day.

Colours in Islam

The colour green has a special place in Islam, and many mosques and Islamic buildings are painted green.

In the Qur'an (Surah 18:31), it is said that in Heaven everyone will wear green clothes made of fine silk. So, artists may sometimes use the colour green to stand for Heaven.

The colour white can stand for purity and peace (one of the meanings of Islam is peace). Many Muslims specifically wear the colour white when they attend Friday prayers. During the pilgrimage to Mecca, each pilgrim wears special clothes made of white cloth.

For some Muslims, the colour black stands for mourning and may be used as a reminder of the death of ancient Muslim leaders, such as the death of the son-in-law of Mohammed (pbuh).

Religious buildings

You can sometimes see images of important religious buildings, such as the Ka'ba and the Dome of the Rock, on Islamic art. Muslims believe that the Ka'ba, in modern day Saudi Arabia, was originally built by Adam, the first human, as the first place to worship God.

Weblink: www.CurriculumVisions.com

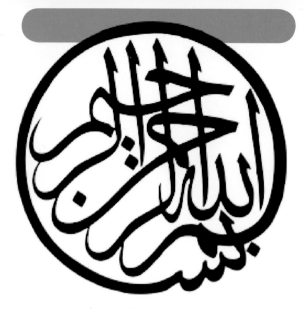

▲ A calligraphy design of the bismillah

Words as symbols

Many Islamic decorations are made up of the words Bismillah ir-Rahman ir-Rahim, which, in English, means "In the name of Allah, the Compassionate, the Merciful". These are the first words in every chapter of the Qur'an.

Many Muslims say these words, or the shorter version, "Bismillah", before doing things like eating, sleeping, praying, doing work or going on a trip.

When verses from the Qur'an, or words such as Allah (God) and Mohammed (pbuh) are written on everyday objects, it also helps to make those objects more important. For example, when a lamp has the phrase "Allah is great" written on it, you are reminded of God every time you turn on the lamp and see the words lit up.

▼ This small prayer rug has a design of a mosque on it.

▼ The prayer rug in this mosque has a design that points the way to Mecca.

The mihrab

Some Muslim monuments and important buildings have arched doorways or gateways leading into the building. These arches may be used to stand for the mihrab in the mosque, which is on the wall facing Mecca. The mihrab and the arch shape stand for the belief that the Islamic faith is the gateway to Heaven.

Prayer rugs

Prayer rugs are used by Muslims to cover the bare ground or floor while they pray. Prayer rugs usually have a design on one end that stands for the prayer niche, or mihrab. This part of the rug is pointed towards Mecca during prayer.

Prayer rugs sometimes have other symbols as decoration or as reminders of faith. For example, rugs may have pictures of the Al-Aqsa mosque, lamps, words or the Crescent Moon on them.

Weblink: www.CurriculumVisions.com

Making art with words

One popular type of Islamic art involves using words.

In Islam, words and sayings from the Qur'an are often used to make Muslim works of art. By changing the shape and size of the words and letters, artists can make words look beautiful, add special meanings to words or emphasise the importance of certain words.

The art of writing to make words look beautiful and to give them extra meaning is called calligraphy. Because it can be used to write the word of God, calligraphy is considered one of the most important types of Islamic art.

◀▼ The inscription on this gateway invites the reader to enter paradise. It has been turned into art and makes up the border around the gateway and beyond the floral decoration.

On pages 26 to 27 you will find pictures of the Taj Mahal, India, and on every surface there is calligraphy.

▲▼ Copies of the Qur'an and other religious books. The decoration on the outside shows you that these books are important.

Arabic alphabet

Islamic calligraphy uses the Arabic alphabet. This is the language that God used to speak to Mohammed (pbuh) and the language the Qur'an is written in.

The Arabic alphabet has 26 letters and is written from right to left. The short vowels are not written next to the consonants, like in English, but are written above or below them.

Just like there are many different styles of typing and writing used in English, there are also many different ways to write Arabic. Some are plain and are used for everyday writing, and some are very fancy and are used mostly in works of art and calligraphy.

The Qur'an

The Qur'an is the holy book of Islam. Ever since the very first copies of the Qur'an were written down, Islamic writers and calligraphers have tried to make the words look as beautiful as possible. This is one way of showing respect and love for the words in the Qur'an.

In many copies of the Qur'an, not only are the words written in a way that makes them look attractive but they are also surrounded by designs and drawings that make the page look beautiful too, and turn it into a work of art.

Where can you find calligraphy?

Calligraphy is not only used on books and paintings. Many Islamic artists use calligraphy to decorate pottery, stone or wood carvings, glass lamps and tiles. In fact, calligraphy can be used anywhere an artist wants to show meaning with words. Many of the objects used in mosques, such as tile decorations, rugs, lamps and even furniture, have calligraphy on them showing verses of the Qur'an.

In mosques, verses from the Qur'an might be used as a single work of art. For example, a verse might be painted on a wall. Sometimes single words, such as Allah or Mohammed (pbuh), are repeated and arranged into patterns over the entire surface of the walls.

Calligraphy is not just a decoration. The words help people to worship. Worshippers are surrounded by the word of God and are reminded of the lessons and ideals of Islam.

The story of Mustafa Rakim

The 17th century Turkish artist, Mustafa Rakim, invented a new way to turn Arabic words into art.

Rakim was unhappy with the way that calligraphy looked. He felt that it was too lifeless and not enough like beautiful art. He wanted to find a way to make calligraphy more beautiful and lifelike.

After many years of work, he developed a style of using words to make pictures. He would sometimes even make letters look like people. For example, he would use the letter aleph ﺍ (makes the same sound as the letter A in English) to stand for a tall person. Another letter, the ayin ﻉ could stand for eyebrows raised in surprise.

Rakim became so famous for his work that the Turkish king, Sultan Mahmud II, would stand in front of him while he worked and hold his inkpot.

Because of this, a new way of making art using words was invented. Some calligraphers form the words into geometric shapes, like circles or squares, and others form the words into the shape of animals or plants.

◄ Words drawn to look like an elephant.

▶ Calligraphy around an arch on the Taj Mahal, Agra, India.

The art of architecture

In Islam, architecture is not only about building useful buildings, but also about making buildings beautiful and about showing faith.

▲ The dome on a mosque helps sound to travel.

The mosque is the centre of worship and of the Muslim community. So, many mosques and other public buildings are designed to remind worshippers of some of the ideals and history of the Muslim faith.

The minaret and dome

Most mosques have tall towers, called minarets. Originally, the main function of the minaret was to provide a place for a man called the muezzin to stand and remind people of when it was time to worship by saying the call to prayer. The tall towers would carry his voice all over the neighbourhood and people would know it was time for one of the five daily prayers. Today, many mosques use loudspeakers instead, but the towers are a constant reminder to people of the daily prayer.

The tall, thin, straight shape of the minaret may also be designed to

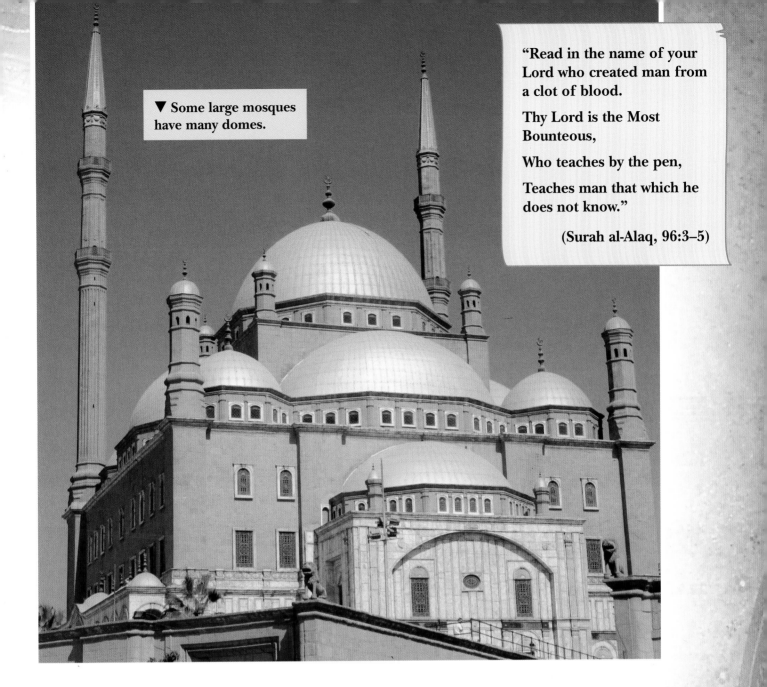

▼ Some large mosques have many domes.

"Read in the name of your Lord who created man from a clot of blood.

Thy Lord is the Most Bounteous,

Who teaches by the pen,

Teaches man that which he does not know."

(Surah al-Alaq, 96:3–5)

look like a pen or the letter aleph ‍ا – the first letter of the Arabic alphabet, like the letter 'A' in English. This may remind people of the first part of the Qur'an that God gave to Mohammed (pbuh) – to read and learn about God:

"Read in the name of your Lord who created man from a clot of blood. Thy Lord is the Most Bounteous, Who teaches by the pen, Teaches man that which he does not know." (Surah al-Alaq, 96:3-5).

Many mosques are built with domes on top. Originally, the shape of the domes helped to carry the voice of the imam, so everyone could hear the sermon, and also kept the mosque cool in the summer. Today, the dome is a reminder of the history of Islam. The high, curved ceiling draws the eyes upward and may also be a reminder of the heavens and of God. This is similar to the tall roofs of many churches.

Weblink: www.CurriculumVisions.com

◄▲ The Taj Mahal, India, – widely recognised as one of the most beautiful buildings in the world – is covered entirely with Islamic art. It is a mausoleum, a tomb, and has many of the decorative effects found in Islamic religious buildings.

Other parts of the mosque

Most mosques have two separate entrances – one for women and one for men. They also have separate areas of worship for men and women. This is a reminder of the importance of modesty in Islam.

Mosques also have a place for worshippers to wash before prayer. This is because everyone is required to wash in a certain way, called wudu, before prayer.

You will notice that the prayer hall, the main part of the mosque, is usually made up of one large open space, sometimes with a separate area for women. This is because everyone worships together.

The prayer room is also usually square or rectangular in shape. This is because Muslims line up in rows to pray, and this is easiest to do in a square or rectangular shaped room. The single open room and lining up in rows are reminders of the Islamic ideal of equality. No one is higher or lower than anyone else.

Many traditional mosques have courtyards, often with water fountains and trees or other plants in them.

▼ The courtyard at the Mohammed Ali mosque in Cairo, Egypt.

▼ Coloured lamps, decorated lights and even candles are also used in many mosques. The light adds beauty and is also a reminder of the light of God.

This is a place for people to gather and socialise and helps to give the idea of the mosque as a centre of the community, and not only a place for worship. The water also serves a practical purpose. As it evaporates, it helps to cool the air and provides a cool place for people to gather.

Islam began in the desert, where water and flowering plants were rare, so the courtyard was also a reminder of the garden paradise of Heaven.

You can see that the design of the mosque tells us a lot about Islamic ideals and faith.

Types of decoration used in mosques

Making mosques look beautiful shows respect and love for God. Geometric patterns and designs can also add a feeling of space inside the mosque.

In traditional mosques, it was common for the men's and women's areas to be separated by a wooden screen in which designs had been carved. The designs allowed the women to see out but did not allow men to see in. These are not used very often today, but some mosques have carved screens as a reminder of this tradition.

Another traditional work of art is a wooden stand for the Qur'an. In many mosques, the prayer room is also used to give lessons in the Arabic language and in the Qur'an. Because there is no furniture in the prayer room, these stands are used for holding copies of the Qur'an during lessons.

Music for worship

Music used in Muslim worship does not usually use instruments.

Islamic songs are songs that have a religious theme or idea. Most Islamic music is sung without any instruments, or uses only simple instruments like drums. This is because some Muslims do not believe that instruments should be used in religious music. So, instead of singing songs accompanied by instruments, most of the music that is used for worship consists of chants or verses of the Qur'an that are sung without musical instruments.

Because they are not accompanied by musical instruments, these songs help listeners to think about the words and their meaning.

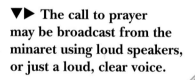

▼▶ The call to prayer may be broadcast from the minaret using loud speakers, or just a loud, clear voice.

The call to prayer

The first Islamic songs were the call to prayer, called the Adhan. This was sung from the tops of minarets five times each day in order to tell people when it was time for prayer. (In many mosques today, however, the Adhan is sung from inside the mosque.) The person who sings the call to prayer is called the muezzin. The muezzin tries to make the words sound as beautiful as possible. The words are always the same (see below).

Words to the call to prayer

Allahu Akbar
God (Allah) is Great *(said four times)*

Ashhadu an la ilaha illa Allah
I bear witness that there is no god
except God (Allah). *(said two times)*

Ashadu anna Muhammadan Rasool Allah
I bear witness that Mohammed
is the messenger of God. *(said two times)*

Hayya 'ala-s-Salah
Hurry to the prayer *(said two times)*

Hayya 'ala-l-Falah
Hurry to success *(said two times)*

For the pre-dawn (fajr) prayer, the following phrase is added here:

As-salatu Khayrun Minan-nawm
Prayer is better than sleep *(said two times)*

Allahu Akbar
God (Allah) is Great *(said two times)*

La ilaha illa Allah
There is no god except God (Allah)

Chanting the Qur'an

Another type of music that is used in worship is chanting verses of the Qur'an. This is done using rhythms and tones so that the words seem like a song. When reciting the Qur'an, there are rules that must be followed, for example, when to pause between words and sentences and how long to pause.

Other music used in worship

Another type of singing used in worship is called madh (pronounced *mad-h*) chanting. Madh are poems in praise of the Prophet Mohammed (pbuh) and they are usually recited during festivals that celebrate Mohammed's (pbuh) birthday.

Another type of chant is called a dhikr. These chants repeat over and over the 99 names of God or a short phrase from the Qur'an, such as La ilaha illa Allah (There is no God but God). Chanting the same thing over and over helps the person doing the chanting, and the people listening, to feel closer to God.

Nasheeds are songs with religious meaning that are sung at festivals and holidays. They are usually accompanied only by a drum.

▼ These children are singing nasheeds and mahds at a festival to celebrate Mohammed's (pbuh) birthday.

Index

Abu Bakr 14
Adhan 30
Al Aqsa mosque 19
Arabic 21, 22, 23, 25, 29

Bismillah 18
black 17

calligraphy 2, 20–23
carving 11, 22
chant 2, 31
circle 8, 22
coconut 10
Crescent Moon 16, 19
Cypress 10

dome 24
Dome of the Rock 17

faith 4
flower 10

Garden of Eden 10

geometric 2, 6, 7, 10, 11, 12, 15, 22, 29
green 10, 17

Heaven 8, 10, 17, 25, 29
hexagon 8

Imam 2, 25
Islam 2 *and throughout*

Ka'ba 2, 17

leaves 10

Madh 31
Mecca 8, 9, 15, 19
mihrab 2, 15, 19
minaret 2, 24
Mohammed (pbuh) 2, 4, 10, 14, 17, 18, 20, 25, 31
mosaic 2, 12–15
mosque 2, 4, 11, 14, 15, 17, 19, 22, 24, 25, 28, 29
muezzin 2, 24, 30

Muslim 2 *and throughout*

painting 4
palm tree 10
peony 10
pilgrimage 2, 17
plant 10, 12, 16
pray 8
prayer rug 19

Qur'an 2, 17, 18, 20, 21, 23, 25, 29, 30, 31

sculpture 4
star 8, 9, 16
symbol 2, 16–18
symmetry 7

Taj Mahal 2, 20, 26–27
tile 12–14, 22

white 17
wudu 2, 28

Curriculum Visions

There's much more on-line including videos

You will find multimedia resources covering six different religions, as well as history, geography, science and spelling subjects in the subscription Professional Zone at:

www.CurriculumVisions.com

A CVP Book
Copyright Earthscape © 2008

Author
Lisa Magloff, MA

Religious Adviser
Iqbal Turk, chairman, the Sunni Muslim Association, London.

Senior Designer
Adele Humphries, BA

Editor
Gillian Gatehouse

Acknowledgements
The publishers would like to thank everyone at the Sunni Muslim Association, London; London Islamic Cultural Society and mosque.

Photographs
All pictures are from the Earthscape and ShutterStock collections.

Designed and produced by
Earthscape

Printed in China by
WKT Company Ltd

Muslim art and writing
– *Curriculum Visions*
A CIP record for this book is available from the British Library
ISBN: 978 1 86214 250 3

This product is manufactured from sustainable managed forests. For every tree cut down at least one more is planted.